SING!
PLAY!
LEARN!

WITH

GO
KID MUSIC

BY AL START

ILLUSTRATIONS BY CHLOE BATCHELOR

"What a lovely voice Al Start has, and I love the way she uses real instruments to accompany her songs" **Julia Donaldson**

Author Acknowledgements

I couldn't have made the songs, music or attempted this first adventure into publishing a book without lots of support; I'd like to thank…

My wonderful partner Cheryl for her love and amazing support, especially during the many long months spent creating this songbook. My daughter TM – this is for you, so one day your kids will have something great to sing at school! My amazing sisters, Catherine and Cheryl who are always there for me come rain or shine. All my lovely friends. Phoebe Bazzard for her excellent camera work and being my right-hand woman, and all the team (past and present) at Go Kid Music. The talented musicians who played on many of the songs and in my band: Deb Shurvell (mandolin, harmonies), Carol Levi (banjo, guitars and bouzouki), Emily Johnson (bass, harmonies), Michael Allardyce (percussion), Bill Melis (drums), Nathan Williams (electric guitar, bass, drums and programming on 'The Dinosaur Dance' – with additional thanks to Mark Flannery at 3Fire). Chloë Batchelor for her fantastic illustrations and for sticking with me over the years! More please!

Helen McGregor for her advice and guidance in putting this collection together, her astounding musical know-how and for all those hours of listening to my songs. Naomi, Mary and the team at HarperCollins for making this happen. My coach and business mentor, Claire James from Pivotal Moment who helped me find the courage to approach publishers in the first place, and her continued support on this rollercoaster ride. A big thanks to Entrepreneurial Spark and all those at Natwest Business Accelerator for the amazing business support and guidance, especially my long-suffering mentor Elena Birchall for her good humour in the face of my apparent lack of business savvy! We got there in the end! All the teachers, support staff and colleagues at the many primary schools at which I have worked, for giving me the opportunity to sing and write songs for all kinds of topics. Special thanks to St Luke's Primary School, Brighton, where it all started. And not forgetting all the children who have sung with me over the years, giving me honest feedback and wild enthusiasm in equal measure! Let's keep on singing!

Al Start

First published 2018
Published by Collins, an imprint of
HarperCollinsPublishers Ltd
The News Building
1 London Bridge Street
London
SE1 9GF
www.collins.co.uk

© 2018 Al Start
10 9 8 7 6 5 4 3 2 1
ISBN: 978-0-00-831822-2

Printed by Caligraving Ltd, Thetford, Norfolk
Designed by Fresh Lemon Australia
Cover and internal illustrations by Chloe Batchelor

Contents

Introduction

Welcome! You've chosen a great songbook to get your children singing and signing, and to give a creative, musical boost to your Key Stage 1 topic work.

Our materials will support you in delivering a fantastic music session with no musical training or background necessary at all – so let me take the hard work and worry out of the equation for you!

My name's Al Start. I'm a singer-songwriter from Brighton, UK with over 30 years' experience of working creatively with children with and without special needs. I have been writing songs for and with children since 2004, having transitioned from being a regular touring singer-songwriter into the world of children's music!

It's a long story, but you can watch my video on my website at **www.gokidmusic.com** to find out all about how it went down. Suffice to say, I found my calling! Our mission at Go Kid Music is to create great songs for children to sing that are age-appropriate and packed with interesting melodies and contemporary music styles that sound good to children and adults alike.

This collection offers you a brilliant selection of popular curriculum-based songs along with simple teaching notes, some cool ideas for further musical and curriculum learning, and brilliant teaching videos. On the videos you'll see me demonstrating the songs with Makaton signs, and lyrics run across the bottom of the screen so the children can sing along. There are often simple instrument/percussion parts that can be added to the songs, offering an easy way to extend musical learning beyond singing. I've also put together some warm-up ideas – I've made recommendations in the song notes, but you can dip into these at any time!

If your school uses Makaton and you're familiar with this visual language support system, you'll be well away! If signing is new to you, do try using this method to teach the songs: you'll be truly amazed at the speed at which children can learn the songs, and it can help them retain the

information for longer. It is inclusive and enjoyable for children with and without learning disabilities, hearing impairments or SEND. Plus, they are learning a valuable communication tool – as are you! So don't be shy: join in and learn alongside the children, and you will reap the rewards! See the 'Makaton' section for more guidance.

WARMING UP

I've put together a selection of warm-ups and listening games that I have learned along the way. You can find these in a PDF on the DVD. Many colleagues, teachers and music practitioners have devised and developed these and have kindly shared them. If you have no musical experience, don't panic: you can do this!

Follow my suggestions and ideas and remember: it's all about the children's experience. If you laugh and have a go, they will too. If you get it wrong but keep trying, so will they. The most important thing is that all adults present join in; even one adult just sitting and watching will give children a negative message, so let all your team know their job is to join in too. No excuses!

Children may be nervous about singing, too. There are many ways of joining in, so please allow your students to develop their confidence over a few weeks. If children tend to misbehave or show off, they are probably feeling anxious. Allow children to watch from the sidelines if they appear nervous – if they know they can join in when they are ready, they will be far more likely to do so than if you force them to join in from the beginning. This is your chance to encourage the start of children's life-long relationship with music, so be gentle and understanding and you will see magic happen before your eyes!

WHY BOTHER?

A few minutes spent focusing your group, warming them up vocally and physically so they won't strain their voices or hurt themselves will also prepare them mentally. It will:

★ break the ice, building a sense of teamwork and trust

★ improve concentration and learning

★ help develop listening skills and cooperation

★ enable you to get to know the group as individuals and observe their development

★ identify children who may need extra support or those with particular ability

★ build the children's experience of being part of a group and all participating in their own way.

These activities can also:

★ rescue your lesson if things aren't working

★ re-focus if you want to change between activities

★ be a fun ending to your session.

DESKS? CHANGE THE SPACE

It's a good idea to prepare the surroundings for a music lesson. If you are in a room with desks, move them to the sides and create a space where everyone can come together. This encourages participation and sets the scene, mentally preparing the students for music time.

TEACHING AND LEARNING THE SONGS

★ Each song comes with:

(i) a teaching video that demonstrates the singing, signing and any instrumental/ percussion parts

(ii) lyric sheets (including separate PDFs on the DVD)

(iii) performance and backing audio tracks

(iv) detailed guidance on how to teach the song.

A full list of resources for each song is provided on the song notes pages.

★ The notes are broken down into sections:

  ★ **Let's Get Started** – Gives you a 'way in' to the song and warm-up suggestions

  ★ **SING!** – Step-by-step instructions on how to teach the song

  ★ **PLAY!** – Shows you how you can extend musical learning, often through adding instruments, body percussion or additional vocal parts, or by refining your singing

  ★ **LEARN!** – Creative ideas to support learning across the curriculum

★ The goal is for the children to learn and internalise the song melody, words, signs and any percussion or instrument parts. Once children have achieved this with the aid of the teaching video, you can swap the video for the audio performance or backing track!

CALL AND RESPONSE

★ I suggest using the 'call and response' method for teaching the songs. This is where you demonstrate a line or phrase of the song (using the signs at the same time), then ask the children to copy this back to you. You can also use the teaching video – just pause and play for each line of the song.

★ By breaking up the song, you can see whether children have got the correct tune/rhythm/ words/signs – and you can correct them before any errors 'stick'. It will become easier the more you do it, and the children will quickly get into the swing of learning in this way.

★ After learning a section, always go back and sing it through a couple of times before moving on to the next part of the song. If you have limited time, you can learn a song over more than one session.

PERCUSSION AND INSTRUMENT PARTS

★ The videos often include some simple instrument parts you can add to your song for deeper musical learning. Why not reach your music attainment targets while you teach your topic! (You can see an overview of the songs and attainment targets in the curriculum grid on page 56.)

★ Always learn the song before adding instrumental parts: as children watch the video to learn the song, they will also be following the percussion parts without realising.

★ To learn the instrument or percussion parts, split the group and allocate each subgroup an instrument and colour name (corresponding to the appropriate coloured window in the video). Teach one percussion/instrument part at a time.

★ For many of the songs, a PDF 'percussion grid' or graphic score is available on the DVD. You can display or print these out and use them to help explain how the rhythm patterns work.

★ Let the children watch the video and copy their part. Observe them closely and make a note of any places where they played for too long, or didn't quite get the beats right. Then go over the video and pause/play/repeat any bits that they need to focus on. Add in the second part (if there is one) in the same way, then play together with each group simply following their own colour-coded window on the video. I have added visual count-ins and GO/STOP signs to help.

★ The 'arrangements' (when instruments start and stop playing) demonstrate just one of many options, so do feel free to experiment!

★ The instruments I have used are also only a guide: use what you have available. Body percussion is a good alternative, e.g. finger clicks, claps, patting laps/chest, stamping feet. Or improvise with items you already have in the classroom (pencils/pens/paintbrushes, chairs, tables, pen pots, etc.) Both options work well as a substitute for any untuned percussion part, e.g. drum, wood blocks. It also doesn't matter which way the children hold the instruments (right- or left-handed) – just do what's comfortable!

MAKATON

★ Makaton is a way of aiding communication using visual signs to support your speech. It is based on British Sign Language (BSL) but, unlike BSL, it is signed alongside speech and in the same order as the words you speak. Only the key words are signed. Traditionally this is used with people with learning disabilities and SEND. To find out more about Makaton, visit the Makaton Charity website **www.makaton.org.uk**

★ A spoken word with a visual cue is also a type of kinaesthetic learning, and there is something quite magical about this approach. There's plenty of evidence to back up the benefits of kinaesthetic learning: it enables many children to learn the facts faster and retain them for longer.

★ Signing while you sing has the added bonuses of being brilliant fun, giving more meaning to a song, engaging children more and adding another creative layer to singing.

★ In the videos I lead with my right hand as I am right-handed. Anyone right-handed should do the same; but if you are left-handed, lead with that and follow the videos as if looking in the mirror.

★ Signs should be accessible to children with both learning disabilities and hearing impairments. I have developed the songs' signs from my background in *Makaton* and *British Sign Language* (BSL), and many of the signs are

based on BSL. You may see a sign I use that you sign differently, so feel free to edit and replace the signs to suit your school. I have also used artistic licence to convey the meaning of the song – so again, follow my signs for the 'author's' version, and swap to your own if need be.

Finally, if you like the songs in this book, you can find more online at **www.gokidmusic.com**!

Enjoy!
Al Start

BIG RED BARN

TOPIC: Farms and farm animals

CROSS-CURRICULAR LINKS: Mathematics, Art & Design, Science

This funny, up-tempo song about a party on a farm is ideal for younger children in Key Stage 1 and EYFS. It counts down from number 10 to 1 and names the animals found on a farm. The signs that accompany the song will enable the staff and children to learn all the Makaton vocabulary for this topic. There are sound effects and noises a-plenty, and opportunities to make funny faces, sounds and actions!

MUSICAL LEARNING

★ Singing in unison
★ Exploring dynamics (volume)
★ Making a range of different sounds with voices
★ Playing untuned instruments to a steady beat

RESOURCES REQUIRED

★ Teaching video
★ Performance track, backing track
★ Lyrics sheet (PDF), warm-ups sheet (PDF)
★ Optional: shakers

LET'S GET STARTED...

★ To introduce the song, play the teaching video to your group. Are you all able to start joining in with the chorus as the song progresses?

★ Ask the children what animal signs they can remember. Discuss any words or phrases the children may not be familiar with; for example, do they know the 'Hokey Cokey'? If not, this is a great opportunity to teach it to them!

WARM-UP

★ Make sure your singers are sitting or standing up straight, with good posture to allow them to breathe well.

★ Choose two or three warm-ups from the PDF to help everyone to focus and get ready to sing!

AL RECOMMENDS...

LISTENING GAME 1: Follow the conductor – a simple, attention-grabbing watching and listening exercise to focus your group.

VOCAL WARM-UP 2: Drive the car – travel up high and down low in your car/truck/motorcycle, making 'brmm' sound effects to stretch mouths and faces. Why not theme this game and play 'Drive the tractor'!

PHYSICAL WARM-UP 3: Wobbly chicken – a funny warm-up to get children moving and thinking about rhythm and pulse.

SING!

★ After warming up, play the track again and encourage the children to join in with the chorus and copy the signs while they sing.

★ Start by teaching the chorus as a call and response (see p. 6).

★ Once secure, sing twice through and then learn the verses in the same way.

★ As the song has many verses, you could learn new verses over two or three sessions. Remind yourselves of the parts you already know before moving on to new verses.

TIP

The signs in the chorus come quickly, (big – red – barn). Practise the hand shapes and ensure the children are opening their mouths and clearly enunciating the words as they sign. Ensure all the adults in the room are also joining in – it is very important for children to see that we are all learning together.

PLAY!

★ If you want to add another layer of sound to the music, shakers would sound great! You can play them on the beat (1, 2, 3, 4) throughout the song.

★ To make it more challenging, direct children to play in the choruses only, stopping on the word 'beg<u>un</u>'. Watch the teaching video to see how this works.

★ Use the last verse with its singing goats and sleeping mouse to introduce the concept of dynamics (volume). Ask the children to explore changing the volume of their voices and their posture when singing these lines: big and loud for the goats; small and quiet for the mouse.

LEARN!

★ Art & Design: If you have a large group, the children could be grouped into animals for a wonderful sharing assembly. Make simple hats or costumes to wear and have each group stand or step forward for the appropriate lyrics when performing. The children could create a lovely class frieze showing the appropriate numbers of animals in the song.

★ Science: If you visit a farm as part of your topic, you may wish to sing the song on the way, or practise the signs along with the names as children are introduced to the real animals. You could also have a game of *Guess the animal* by demonstrating the signs and asking the children to identify the creature. This could be expanded into a discussion about what the animal looks like and where it lives.

AL SAYS

"What other farm-based songs and nursery rhymes can the children sing using the signing vocabulary from this song? Once you have learned your animal signs, 'Old MacDonald' will look better than ever!"

BIG RED BARN

(Introduction)

VERSE 1

There were ten cows munching on grass,
Nine sheep doing a dance. (woo-hoo!)
They did the hokey-cokey and they turned around,
And that's what it's all about! Hey!

CHORUS

Down on the farm in the big red barn,
There's singing and music and fun.
Down on the farm in the big red barn,
The summer party's begun!

VERSE 2

There were eight hens laying an egg, (pop!)
Seven ducks with hats on their heads. (mmm!)
They put their left wing in and their left wing out,
And they were shaking it all about! Hey!

CHORUS

Down on the farm in the big red barn,
There's singing and music and fun.
Down on the farm in the big red barn,
The summer party's begun!

VERSE 3

There were six little chicks eating Weetabix,
Five fat pigs in the mud. (Splat!)
They did a squelch and a belch as they turned around,
And that's what it's all about! Hey!

CHORUS

Down on the farm in the big red barn,
There's singing and music and fun.
Down on the farm in the big red barn,
The summer party's begun!

VERSE 4

There were four cats looking for mice, (squeak!)
Three grumpy donkeys trying to be nice.
They put their tail in and their tail out,
And they were shaking it all about! Hey!

CHORUS

Down on the farm in the big red barn,
There's singing and music and fun.
Down on the farm in the big red barn,
The summer party's begun!

VERSE 5

There were two goats singing out of tune, (bleeeeat!)
One little mouse asleep in a shoe. (sssshhh)
The farmer and his wife, they've lived here all their life,
They say that's what it's all about! Hey!

FINAL CHORUS

Down on the farm in the big red barn,
There's singing and music and fun.
Down on the farm in the big red barn,
The summer party's begun!
The summer party's begun!

THE DINOSAUR DANCE

TOPIC: Dinosaurs, fossils and the museum

CROSS-CURRICULAR LINKS: Physical Education, Science

A rhythmic, funny song that is easy to learn, teach and sing – perfect for young children. The signs are nice and easy and there are a range of different sounds children can make using their voices. This song can be sung sitting down or can be used to get everyone up dancing – great for reluctant singers.

MUSICAL LEARNING

★ Making a range of sounds with voices
★ Singing in unison
★ Playing untuned instruments musically

RESOURCES REQUIRED

★ Teaching video
★ Performance track, backing track
★ Lyrics sheet (PDF), warm-ups sheet (PDF)
★ Optional: percussion, e.g. drums, wood blocks, tambourines, percussion grid (PDF)

LET'S GET STARTED...

★ To introduce the song, play the teaching video/performance track to your group. Do they recognise any key facts from their learning of the topic so far? Can they name the dinosaurs in the song (e.g. Diplodocus, Brontosaurus)?

★ Discuss any words or phrases the children may not be familiar with; for example, what does 'tall and lanky' mean? What is a hankie? In verse 2, what does the line 'squash you like a pancake, can you feel the earthquake?' mean? (The Mammoth is so big he'd squash you if he trod on you, and the ground shakes when he stomps along!)

WARM-UP

★ Make sure your singers are sitting or standing up straight, with good posture to allow them to breathe well.

★ Choose two or three warm-ups from the PDF to help everyone to focus and get ready to sing!

AL RECOMMENDS...

LISTENING GAME 2: Don't clap this one back – a short, snappy listening exercise to grab everyone's attention.

VOCAL WARM-UP 4: The moody song – singing a familiar song in a range of moods, e.g. sleepy/angry/bored/excited. Make sure everyone stretches their mouths and faces.

PHYSICAL WARM-UP 3: Wobbly chicken – a funny warm-up to get children moving and thinking about rhythm and pulse.

AL SAYS

" Don't worry if you have different instruments to those in the examples. Claves or any type of block will work for the wood block part, and any kind of box, bongo, drum, tambour (with skin) will work for the drum part. Have fun mixing and matching different instruments! "

SING!

★ After warming up, play the teaching video again. Can the children copy the signs and join in for the chorus?

★ The children will automatically want to stamp their feet on the words, 'stamp your feet on the ground', so remind them that we use our hands to sign and not our feet. (If you are adding dance movement to the song, invite them to stamp their feet for the Dinosaur Dance at the end; otherwise, use hands on knees throughout as in the teaching video.)

★ Teach the chorus using the call-and-response method (see p. 6). On the video/track, we've emphasised the wordplay, e.g. 'saw us' sounds like 'saur-us', but you may prefer to keep the 'w' sound.

★ Sing through the chorus at least twice before moving on to the verses to make sure your group is able to sing and sign the words correctly. Teach the verses in the same way, then sing through the whole song.

★ Encourage everyone to be expressive with their body and face as well as their voice. Play the track through, focusing on the funny bits; have fun with the children sneezing, getting covered in dinosaur bogies and stamping, raaaaaahhing, etc. Then incorporate this into the singing.

★ Finish the song with a final giant dinosaur 'raaaaaaaaahh!'.

TIP

Explain to the children how long you want the 'raaaaahhing' to last, how loud it should be and what to do after it – e.g. sit up straight with their hands in their laps in silence for the end of the song. Agree a visual cue (such as raising your hand) that you will use to signal for them to stop.

PLAY!

★ This song has a strong, clear pulse that is ideal to get children counting beats and playing percussion.

★ There are two percussion parts shown on the teaching video – watch to see how they work together. You can also refer to the PDF percussion grid.

★ The drum plays on the first beat of each bar, while the wood block plays on the second and fourth beats. Ask the children to count along to the music and clap on their beats: drummers should clap on 1 only and wood blocks on 2 and 4. Repeat, this time with instruments.

★ You can explore different 'arrangements' by having the instruments play at different times – we have the wood block playing throughout and the drum playing in the choruses, middle 8 and outro. Try a few options together and decide which one you like best.

★ We've created interest by adding hits on 'Hey!' in the verses and having the wood block playing on 'next' at the end of the choruses then having a short break before the next verse. Watch out for the extra hits and 'rattles' at the end of the verses too!

★ Alternatively, you could use body percussion: the children could stamp, clap or tap along with the percussion parts.

LEARN!

★ Science: Ask the children to choose one of the four creatures mentioned in the song and create a fact file including a drawing and information on their size, habitat and what they liked to eat.

★ Physical Education (dance): Get active and do the Dinosaur Dance at the end – just follow the instructions in the lyrics!

THE DINOSAUR DANCE

(Introduction)

VERSE 1
Hocus Pocus, the scary Diplodocus,
Lives in the museum.
Hey! Have you seen him?
Tall and lanky, never has a hankie,
Sneezing all of the time,
Watch out for the green slime! (Aa-aa-aa-choo!)

CHORUS
Louder than a stamping Brontosaurus,
Louder than Tyrannosaurus Rex. (Raaaaaahhhh!)
What d'you think would happen if he saw us? (Uh-oh!)
What would happen next?

VERSE 2
There's Mr McManus, the hairy Woolly Mammoth,
Lives in the museum.
Hey! Have you seen him?
Big and shaggy, grumpy and craggy,
Squash you like a pancake,
Can you feel the earth quake? (Woah!)

CHORUS
Louder than a stamping Brontosaurus,
Louder than Tyrannosaurus Rex. (Raaaaaahhhh!)
What d'you think would happen if he saw us? (Uh-oh!)
What would happen next?

MIDDLE 8

At the Dinosaur Dance, the Dinosaur Dance,
If you get an invite, better jump at the chance.
The Dinosaur Dance, the Dinosaur Dance,
Oh, if you get an invite, better jump at the chance.

OUTRO *(x3)*

Jump up, duck down,
Stamp your feet on the ground,
Kick your leggies like the Steggies
And turn around.

And around and around and around and around and around!

(Raaaaaaaaahh!)

FRIEND TO THE END

TOPIC: Friendship, Anti-Bullying Week

CROSS-CURRICULAR LINKS: Art & Design, PSHE

This chanting song repeats over a rhythmic track and has lots of opportunities for adding percussion parts. Popular with Key Stages 1 and 2, it is ideal as a whole-school assembly song in Anti-Bullying Week.

MUSICAL LEARNING

★ Singing in two parts
★ Playing untuned instruments musically
★ Exploring rhythm/duration

RESOURCES REQUIRED

★ Teaching video, slowed-down teaching video
★ Performance track, backing track
★ Lyrics sheet (PDF), warm-ups sheet (PDF)
★ Optional: percussion (e.g. drums, claves, wood blocks), percussion grid (PDF), percussion video

LET'S GET STARTED...

★ To introduce the song, play the teaching video/performance track to your group.
★ What does 'friend to *the end*' mean to them? Discuss loyalty. What does being a good friend involve?

WARM-UP

★ Make sure your singers are sitting or standing up straight, with good posture to allow them to breathe well.
★ Choose two or three warm-ups from the PDF to help everyone to focus and get ready to sing!

AL SAYS

"Some children may find the song style a little challenging, but there is a lot of repetition, which will help. See if you can add dynamics (volume and energy/power) to gradually build up the song, then quieten down at the end of the last 'very good friend indeed'.
If you perform the song, why not get the audience to join in with shouting out the letters?!"

AL RECOMMENDS...

LISTENING GAME 2: Don't clap this one back – a short, snappy listening exercise to grab everyone's attention.

VOCAL WARM-UP 4: The moody song – singing a familiar song in a range of moods, e.g. sleepy/angry/bored/excited. Make sure everyone stretches their mouths and faces.

PHYSICAL WARM-UP 2: Numbers and letters – draw shapes with different parts of the body.

SING!

★ After warming up, play the track again and encourage the children to join in. Note that the structure is very simple: the verse is sung three times, followed by a section that repeats certain lines and phrases from the verse.

★ Can the children copy the signs for the letters while they sing?

★ Without the music, recap the signs for the letters. Call out each letter slowly at first, then gradually speed up until everyone is confident signing along to the music.

★ Next, learn the lines that follow each letter, using call and response (see p. 6). You could start with the slowed-down teaching video to learn the words and signs first, as these lines move quite quickly.

★ The verse works best if singers are split into two groups: one that chants the letters and one that delivers the lines in between (as in the video).

PLAY!

★ This song is perfect for building up a class percussion ensemble, using instruments and/or body percussion.

★ There is a separate video demonstrating optional percussion parts on drum and claves (also shown in the percussion grid).

★ The drum plays through most of the song, usually on beat 1 (with the chanting of the letters 'F', 'R', etc.). There's an extra hit in the last line of each verse: 'Cos a <u>friend</u> who's a <u>friend</u> to the <u>end</u>...'

★ The claves start after the word 'indeed' at the end of the first verse and stop before 'Cos a friend...', following this pattern for the rest of the verses and continuing through the outro.

★ The claves rhythm is: 1-<u>2</u>-3-<u>&</u>-<u>4</u>.

★ You can play these rhythms on almost any percussion instruments. When you've learned the parts, you can divide into four groups: two singing and signing groups and two percussion groups. Give everyone the opportunity to try each part.

★ Why not invite the children to come up with their own rhythms to play? Break off into pairs or small groups then come together for a sharing session!

★ Once you've learned both parts, split the group and practise them together a few times. Alternatively, leave out the chant and have everyone sing the 'in between bits' together.

★ The last few lines should be sung by everyone: teach these to the group in the same way, then practise the whole verse through, making sure everyone joins in for 'Cos a friend...'

TIP
It may help to note that the melody for the first three phrases (F, R and I) is exactly the same. Watch out for the quick movement between 'Do my loudest cheer' and 'Cos a friend'.

★ The outro is made up of repetitions of the last line of the verse, 'Is a very good friend indeed' and the 'F-R-I-E-N-D' chant. It's quite instinctive, so the best approach is to sing the entire song through a few times with the track until everyone's familiar with the structure.

★ Finally, go back to the beginning and learn the introduction.

TIP
The final 'F-R-I-E-N-D' chant can be sung over the top of the line, 'Is a very good friend indeed' (as demonstrated in the audio). If you have confident singers, some pupils could carry on singing while the others chant.

LEARN!

★ Art & Design: On six large pieces of card, draw an outline for each letter of the word 'FRIEND'. Divide the class into six groups and ask them to work together to decorate the letter allocated to their group using a range of materials. A child could be nominated from each group to hold up the letter at the appropriate moment when you sing the song.

FRIEND TO THE END

Introduction
Ooh, oh, oh yeah, uh-huh-huh

VERSES *(x3)*
F – F is for my friend,
R – really can depend!
I – I am so lucky,
E – everyone can see.
N – Now my friend is here,
D – do my loudest cheer
Cos a friend who's a friend to the end
Is a very good friend indeed!
Yeah, yeah, yeah!

OUTRO
Is a very good friend indeed!
Yeah, yeah, yeah!
A very good friend indeed!
Yeah, yeah, yeah!
A very good friend indeed!

(F – R – I – E – N – D)
Yeah, yeah, yeah!
A very good friend indeed!
Yeah, yeah, yeah!
(slow) You're a very good friend indeed!

GO SANTA GO!

TOPIC: Christmas

CROSS-CURRICULAR LINKS: English, Art & Design

This is a thumping, upbeat Christmas song that is very popular – and in fact requested all year round! It tells the tale of Santa battling against the wind in his sleigh on Christmas Eve. It introduces the concept of opposites and has plenty of actions that will have children up and dancing!

MUSICAL LEARNING

★ Exploring dynamics (volume)
★ Singing with expression
★ Playing untuned instruments to a steady beat

RESOURCES REQUIRED

★ Teaching video
★ Performance track, backing track
★ Lyrics sheet (PDF), warm-ups sheet (PDF)
★ Optional: percussion, e.g. sleigh bells, shakers, tambourines

LET'S GET STARTED...

★ To introduce the song, play the teaching video/performance track to your group.
★ Discuss the meaning of the song and clarify any words or phrases the children may not understand. What other names is Santa known by?
★ Can they remember the sign for Santa? (There are variations, but I have chosen the sign using his sack as it works well in this song and flows with the other signs.)
★ Ask them how to sign up/down, hot/cold and talk about opposites.

WARM-UP

★ Make sure your singers are sitting or standing up straight, with good posture to allow them to breathe well.
★ Choose two or three warm-ups from the PDF to help everyone to focus and get ready to sing!

AL RECOMMENDS...

LISTENING GAME 3: Now be a statue – a fun rhythmic clapping game to focus your group.

VOCAL WARM-UP 4: The moody song – singing a familiar song in a range of moods, e.g. sleepy/angry/bored/excited. Make sure everyone stretches their mouths and faces.

PHYSICAL WARM-UP 3: Wobbly chicken – a funny counting warm-up to get children moving and thinking about rhythm and pulse.

SING!

★ After warming up, play the track again and encourage the children to join in with the chorus. Can they copy the signs while they sing?

★ Teach the chorus one line at a time while demonstrating the signs (using call and response, p. 6).

★ Practise the difference between the signs for 'wind' and 'snow'.

★ Discuss what Santa's sack might contain (this explains how we sign his name).

★ Move on to learning each verse, demonstrating the signs with the words as you go.

★ When singing to the backing track, listen out for the four taps that signal the entry into the verse at 0:08.

TIP
Note that there are some similarities between the words in verse 1 (low/high) and verse 3 (up/down). Ensure you differentiate these with your hand shapes by following the video carefully.

PLAY!

★ Once the children have learned the song words, try adding dynamics (changing the volume). When you warmed up with 'The moody song', did you sing louder for 'angry' and quietly for 'sleepy'? This is a perfect example of dynamics.

★ To allow the children to explore using dynamics with their voices, ask them how they might emphasise different words like hot/cold and hard/soft using both volume and the tone of their voices. Will some words or phrases be spoken rather than sung? Make sure everyone makes a clear distinction between the two.

★ Sleigh bells sound lovely played on the beat in the chorus of this song – see the teaching video for a demonstration. Tambourines or shakers would also work well.

★ Other instruments, body percussion or vocal effects could be used imaginatively to represent some of the key words in the verses (such as 'the wind blew *low,* the wind blew *high*' and 'the wind blew *hard,* the wind blew *soft*').

★ There is no right and wrong with what you and the children choose to play – have fun experimenting and then deciding together what works best for your group.

LEARN!

★ English: In this song, Santa has to battle the wind on Christmas Eve. Can your class think of other things that might stop Santa getting to their chimneys? It could be more weather, a problem with the sleigh or a reindeer, maybe something happens to his sacks of presents? Write a story with a beginning, a middle – where disaster strikes – and a last-minute solution leading to a happy ending.

★ Art & Design: Following on from the above, the children could draw or paint the disaster to add to their story or for a funny festive display.

AL SAYS

" This is a perfect song for a Christmas show or assembly: you could add costumes, a sleigh, reindeer and of course Santa himself! "

GO SANTA GO !

(Introduction)

VERSE 1

The wind got up, the wind got strong,
The wind blew Santa's sleigh along.
The wind blew low, the wind blew high,
It blew that sleigh up in the sky.

CHORUS

You've gotta go, Santa, go!
You've gotta beat that wind, you know.
Cos here comes all the snow:
Go, Santa, go!

VERSE 2

The wind blew hot, the wind blew cold,
The wind made Santa lose his hold. (Woah!)
The wind blew loud, a great big blast.
"Look out Santa – you're going too fast!"

CHORUS

Go, Santa, go!
You've gotta beat that wind, you know.
Cos here comes all the snow:
Go, Santa, go!

VERSE 3

The wind blew up, the wind blew down,
The wind made Rudolph really frown.
The wind blew hard, the wind blew soft.
"Hooray," cried Santa, "I think it's stopped!"

CHORUS *(x2)*

Go, Santa, go!
You've gotta beat that wind, you know.
Cos here comes all the snow:
Go, Santa, go!

I LOVE CAKE!

TOPIC: Cakes and baking

CROSS-CURRICULAR LINKS: Art & Design, English

A catchy, country-style song with a bluegrass feel that's great for whole-school singing as it's loved by children of all ages. This song is a must – just for fun, even if your topic isn't baking! They'll enjoy shouting out, 'not too much!' and the song gets faster and faster to the end, which is as irresistible as cake!

MUSICAL LEARNING

★ Exploring tempo (speed)
★ Singing in unison
★ Playing untuned instruments musically

RESOURCES REQUIRED

★ Teaching video
★ Performance track, backing track
★ Lyrics sheet (PDF), warm-ups sheet (PDF)
★ Optional: percussion instruments or sound-makers that can be shaken, beaten or tapped (e.g. egg shaker, wooden spoons); percussion grid (PDF), long version audio tracks (performance and backing), long version lyrics sheet (PDF)

LET'S GET STARTED...

★ To introduce the song, play the teaching video/performance track to your group.

★ Can they identify the main instrument used on this track? (The banjo) And do they know the style of music? You could play them some traditional Bluegrass or Country music to give them a flavour!

★ Discuss any words or phrases the children may not be familiar with, such as the different types of cakes listed in the verses. Do they enjoy baking at home?

★ Did they notice what happened to the song at the end? (It got faster)

★ Can they show you the sign for cake?

WARM-UP

★ Make sure your singers are sitting or standing up straight, with good posture to allow them to breathe well.

★ Choose two or three warm-ups from the PDF to help everyone to focus and get ready to sing!

AL RECOMMENDS...

LISTENING GAME 3: Now be a statue – a fun rhythmic clapping game to focus your group.

VOCAL WARM-UP 5: Tongue Twisters – get mouths and voices ready for lots of words!

PHYSICAL WARM-UP 3: Wobbly chicken – a funny warm-up to get children moving and thinking about rhythm and pulse.

AL SAYS

"A fun way to start this song is to pretend to 'wash your hands', 'put on aprons' and imagine mixing the ingredients in a big bowl. At the end you can 'eat' your imaginary cakes!"

SING!

★ After warming up, play the track again and encourage the children to join in with the chorus. Can they stir their imaginary bowl and call out, 'not too much!' while they watch?

★ Note that they will want to get louder on 'not too much' – you may have to ask them not to shout in case this distresses some children. Encourage them to 'pretend shout' – i.e. look as though they are shouting while maintaining a reasonable volume!

★ Start by teaching the chorus using call and response (see p. 6) and note that the tune in the second line is slightly different: it goes up on the words 'stuff' and 'little bit of sugar'.

★ When they can confidently sing the chorus, teach the verses in the same way.

★ The middle 8 section ('Oh gimme, gimme, gimme') has a different tune and will need singing through a few times. The signs are quite fast (breakfast, lunch and dinner and tea) so practise these slowly without the backing a few times to allow the children to try them out; then gradually get faster to match the speed of the track.

★ If you're feeling brave, you could attempt the long version of the song, which has three additional verses. The lyrics move too quickly to include signs, but the cake list is lots of fun and a good challenge for the children! The long version audio and lyrics are on the DVD.

★ The ending seems easy as it speeds up, but children will want to race off and go too fast! Encourage them to listen carefully to the backing music and to pay attention to each other so that they sing as a group.

★ When singing to the backing track, listen out for the four taps that signal the entry into the verse at 0:12.

PLAY!

★ Introduce a couple of simple percussion parts. It doesn't matter what you use, but have some things you can shake (egg shakers are good!) and some you can beat or tap (wooden spoons, chopsticks, plastic bowls).

★ Divide the group into two – Shakers and Beaters.

★ Shakers: create a steady rhythm in the chorus by shaking in time with the words 'Eggs and flour and…'. Join in again from the middle 8, and remember to gradually speed up towards the end!

★ Beaters: play in the chorus but with fewer notes than the shakers – starting on the word 'and', e.g. 'Eggs <u>and</u> flour <u>and</u>…' and so on. They also play in time with the words 'not too much'.

★ See the teaching video and/or refer to the percussion grids.

★ If you do not wish to use instruments, you can improvise with clapping hands, clicking fingers, tapping knees or even tables (with caution!)

TIP

You can help them stay in time at the end by clearly mouthing the words and signing at the front – this will give them additional visual cues. It's just a matter of practice: they will get the feel for how fast to go after a few tries.

LEARN!

★ English: Once the children know this song, there is scope for them to write their own words for the chorus. For example, make up words for Halloween (a delicious witches' brew) or change the recipe to something you are making – pizza, salad, etc. Or it could even become a class anthem: 'Reading and writing and learning and stuff, a little bit of talking but… *NOT TOO MUCH!*'

★ Art & Design: Why not draw, paint or make a collage of a delicious and crazy cake to display? What funny ingredients can the children add? Can they label their picture?

I LOVE CAKE!

(Introduction)

VERSE 1
Well, there's one thing I love to do,
It's so easy, you can do it too!
It doesn't take long, not long to make,
What do I love? I love to bake!

CHORUS
**Eggs and flour and butter and stuff,
A little bit of sugar, but not too much!
Eggs and flour and butter and stuff,
A little bit of sugar, but not too much!**

(Interlude)

VERSE 2
Well, there's one thing I love to eat,
It's a yummy little treat!
A slice of heaven on a plate;
What do I love? I love cake!

CHORUS

Eggs and flour and butter and stuff,
A little bit of sugar, but not too much!
Eggs and flour and butter and stuff,
A little bit of sugar, but not too much!

(Interlude)

MIDDLE 8

Oh gimme, gimme, gimme, gimme, gimme that cake!
I'll eat it at work or on a break.
Breakfast, lunch and dinner and tea:
There's never, ever too much cake for me!

CHORUS *(x3, getting faster)*

Eggs and flour and butter and stuff,
A little bit of sugar, but not too much!
Eggs and flour and butter and stuff,
A little bit of sugar, but not too much!

OUTRO *(getting faster, then slower for last line)*

A little bit of sugar, but not too much.
A little bit of sugar, but not too much!

A PIRATE ADVENTURE

TOPIC: Pirates, the sea and sailing

CROSS-CURRICULAR LINKS: Art & Design, Physical Education

A catchy song combining a sea-shanty-style chorus with pirate adventure descriptions in the verses. Plenty of action-packed signs make this energetic song the perfect accompaniment to your Pirate topic. It also works well as a singing assembly favourite. There is the opportunity to add percussion and for children to create sound effects.

MUSICAL LEARNING

★ Singing with expression
★ Playing untuned instruments to a steady beat
★ Exploring and combining sounds

RESOURCES REQUIRED

★ Teaching video
★ Performance track, backing track
★ Lyrics sheet (PDF), warm-ups sheet (PDF)
★ Optional: a range of untuned percussion and beaters, various sound-makers, e.g. rainsticks, homemade shakers

LET'S GET STARTED...

★ To introduce the song, play the teaching video/performance track to your group.
★ Discuss the words and phrases in the lyrics to ensure the children understand the meaning, e.g. what does 'shiver me timbers' mean?
★ Do they recognise any key facts from their learning of the topic so far? What parts of a ship can they name? Can they describe the pirate in the song?

WARM-UP

★ Make sure your singers are sitting or standing up straight, with good posture to allow them to breathe well.
★ Choose two or three warm-ups from the PDF to help everyone to focus and get ready to sing!

AL SAYS

AL RECOMMENDS...

LISTENING GAME 2: Don't clap this one back – a short, snappy listening exercise to grab everyone's attention. Introduce 'Now be a statue' (Listening Game 3) as an adaptation of this.

VOCAL WARM-UP 3: Lady in the lift – practise moving voices up and down like a lift! Make all the sound effects to stretch mouths and faces.

PHYSICAL WARM-UP 5: A four- or eight-beat dance – choose four or eight different moves to go in sequence as you move to a beat or clap along.

" This song makes a brilliant performance piece and is ideal for a sharing assembly with singing, signing and even a band! If you add percussion parts, encourage the children to play sensitively and not too loud – you don't want to drown out the singers! "

SING!

★ After warming up, play the track again and encourage the children to join in with the chorus. Can they copy the signs while they sing?

★ Encourage them to imagine how heavy the anchor might be and to use both their body movement and voice to sing with expression.

★ Can they practise their grumpy pirate face while 'in jail'?

★ Teach the chorus as a call and response (see p. 6), then sing it through twice, making sure everyone's able to sing and sign the words correctly.

★ Learn the verses in the same way. Notice how the words are faster here: you will need to ensure children are sitting upright, breathing well and opening their mouths to get those words out clearly. Encourage them to use pirate expressions to emphasise the dramatic parts!

★ When you have learned a verse, go back and sing it through with the chorus after it, until you have finished the song.

TIP

This song is quite slow – make sure you use strong, whole-body actions to help children feel the beat. Also note that the tempo (speed) of the song sometimes changes; for instance, it slows down at the end of verses. Make sure everyone is listening carefully to the track so that you all keep in time with the music.

PLAY!

★ This song can be accompanied by a simple drum beat during the chorus, as if beating out the time for pirates to haul in the anchor and sails!

★ The beat is a simple '1, 2, 3, 4' and follows the words, 'Oh heave-ho the anchor'. First, try counting '1, 2, 3, 4' along with the chorus. Then distribute your percussion instruments and practise tapping them in time with your counting.

★ Percussion also sounds great in the instrumental section (some quiet vocals can be heard on the track, but these aren't to be sung by the group). You could limit the percussion playing to this section, so the children can really focus on their percussion-playing skills.

★ If percussion instruments are limited, you could create a pattern or patterns with body percussion – this would emphasise the physical theme in the lyrics. The teaching video demonstrates a simple rhythm based on lap taps for 1 and 3, and claps for 2 and 4. Watch out for the single-handed lap taps on '& 3'!

★ Why not explore adding sound effects to create the sounds of the sea? For example, use rainsticks, ocean drums or rice in a plastic bottle (you can hear these on the audio!).

LEARN!

★ Physical Education: Invite your 'pirate crew' of singers to devise a dance for the instrumental section! They could incorporate actions like pulling in the anchor, hoisting the sails and walking the plank.

★ Art & Design: The pirate in the song is searching for gold. Discuss what other things might be considered 'treasure' – perhaps jewellery or modern-day 'treasure' like mobile phones and tablets? Ask each child to draw a piece of treasure to be arranged in a class display – perhaps overflowing from a treasure chest!

A PIRATE ADVENTURE

(Introduction)

VERSE 1

I've got a patch on my eye, a peg for a leg,
A great big hook for a hand.
My whiskers are black as a witch's old cat,
I'm the cleverest pirate in all of the land.
Shiver me timbers, hoist the sail,
Let's head for that terrible weather.
I have a plan, I know just where we can
Find us a pile of treasure.

CHORUS
So oh heave-ho the anchor,
Oh heave-ho the sail.
On our pirate adventure
We're gonna all end up in jail!

VERSE 2
My name is Hook, so take a look
At this map upon the wall.
"X" marks the spot, lads
And I want it all.
So run ashore and find me more,
Don't look at me so blank.
Find me the gold, lads
Or I'll make you walk the plank.

(Instrumental/backing vocals)

CHORUS *(x2)*
Oh heave-ho the anchor,
Oh heave-ho the sail.
On our pirate adventure
We're gonna all end up in jail!

THE SEED AND THE TREE

TOPIC: Plants and growing

CROSS-CURRICULAR LINKS: Science, Art & Design

A beautiful, gentle song with a lovely message that is ideal for young singers. It features simple makaton signs showing the process of planting and growing, and counting to three. Perfect to share in an assembly – there won't be a dry eye in the house!

MUSICAL LEARNING

★ Singing with expression

★ Exploring dynamics (volume)

★ Playing untuned instruments musically

RESOURCES REQUIRED

★ Teaching video

★ Performance track, backing track

★ Lyrics sheet (PDF), warm-ups sheet (PDF)

★ Optional: percussion, e.g. triangles, bells

LET'S GET STARTED...

★ To introduce the song, play the teaching video/performance track to your group.

★ Talk through the lyrics together. What does it mean to 'love your tree'? (Giving the plant what it needs to thrive.) How would they do this? How could they 'keep it warm in winter snow'? And why would they need to?

★ How long would a seed really take to grow into a tree? Years!

WARM-UP

★ Make sure your singers are sitting or standing up straight, with good posture to allow them to breathe well.

★ Choose two or three warm-ups from the PDF to help everyone to focus and get ready to sing!

AL RECOMMENDS...

LISTENING GAME 1: Follow the conductor – a simple, attention-grabbing watching and listening exercise to focus your group.

VOCAL WARM-UP 1: Gobble-de-gook – have a 'chat' with your group in gobble-de-gook! Move your voice up high and down low, checking that everyone makes all the sound effects to stretch their mouths and faces.

PHYSICAL WARM-UP 3: Wobbly chicken – a funny warm-up to get children moving and thinking about rhythm and pulse.

SING!

★ After warming up, play the track again and encourage the children to join in with the counting part. Can they hold up their fingers to count and sign 'see'?

★ Next, teach the song as a call and response (see p. 6). Repeat each verse a couple of times until you are happy that everyone is able to join in. Once secure, sing through the whole song.

★ Notice the different lyrics in the last two sections: '1, 2, 3, you and me' rather than '… you will see'. The children may need reminding of this until they are familiar with the song.

TIP

Invite the children to point to a friend on the words, 'you and me'. If you share the song as a performance, they could point to a family member.

PLAY!

★ Encourage the use of dynamics (loud and soft) to emphasise certain words and phrases. For instance, sing 'a tiny little tree' at the end of verse 1 softly and 'a great big tree' at the end of verse 2 with more volume and power; then maintain this volume for the third and fourth sections.

★ Triangles and/or bells add a lovely, magical feel to this song. Play them at the same time as the words, 'One, two, three' and 'you will see', or 'you and me' in the last verse. Children can follow the teaching video, which shows them when to play.

TIP

Play the video for the song on the whiteboard in your classroom from time to time. The children will pick up the lyrics, tune and even the signs as they play or carry on with other activities. When you next sing the song, they will be even more familiar with it.

LEARN!

★ Science: Encourage the children to imagine gathering all the items they need to plant a seed. Ask them to put on their (imaginary) gardening gloves, get their earth nice and flat, make a hole with their finger, fill their watering cans (using sound effects!), open their seed packet and hold one up, ready to plant. This will help them prepare for the signs and the song, and to think through the planting process.

★ Art & Design: If you are planning to share/ perform this song, you may like to encourage the children to make simple hats with seeds/trees on, which they can wear with green clothes for a performance of the song.

AL SAYS

❝ Another fun physical warm-up is to go through the imaginary preparation of planting a seed, then encourage the children to pretend they are the plant as it grows bigger, bigger… and explodes into a huge tree! You can do this a couple of times with a 'new' seed each time. Extend this into your performance, too: when they sing the last line of the song, they could 'grow' (stand with hands raised as branches) and become a forest! ❞

THE SEED AND THE TREE

(Introduction)

VERSE 1
Plant the seed in the ground,
Sprinkle water all around.

CHORUS 1
1, 2, 3...
You will see
A tiny little tree.

VERSE 2
Love your tree, watch it grow;
Keep it warm in winter snow.

CHORUS 2
1, 2, 3…
And you will see
A great big tree!

BRIDGE
We can climb it,
And hide behind it.
Won't you come with me?

CHORUS 3
1, 2, 3…
You and me
Underneath our tree.

(repeat Bridge and Chorus 3)

SEPTEMBER 1666

TOPIC: The Great Fire of London

CROSS-CURRICULAR LINKS: History, English, Art & Design

A gentle song that tells the story of the Great Fire of London. It has a rousing chorus that sounds brilliant with the optional two-part singing at the end. A great song to get started with part-singing and a perfect alternative to 'London's Burning'!

MUSICAL LEARNING

★ Exploring dynamics (volume)
★ Singing in two parts
★ Playing tuned instruments musically
★ Improvising and composing

RESOURCES REQUIRED

★ Teaching video
★ Performance track, backing track
★ Lyrics sheet (PDF), warm-ups sheet (PDF)
★ Optional: glockenspiel/xylophone/chime bars and beaters, graphic score (PDF)

LET'S GET STARTED...

★ To introduce the song, play the teaching video/performance track to your group. What do they think the song is about? Do they recognise any key facts from their learning of the topic so far?

★ Discuss any words or phrases the children may not be familiar with. For example, what are 'kindling sticks' and how does this relate to the materials houses were built from in 1666? What does the line, 'it was a nightmare they'd been dreading' mean? (There were several big fires in the years leading up to the Great Fire and they feared a really big fire may take hold one day.)

WARM-UP

★ Make sure your singers are sitting or standing up straight, with good posture to allow them to breathe well.

★ Choose two or three warm-ups from the PDF to help everyone to focus and get ready to sing!

AL RECOMMENDS...

LISTENING GAME 2: Don't clap this one back – a short, snappy listening exercise to grab everyone's attention.

VOCAL WARM-UP 3: Lady in the lift – practise moving voices up and down like a lift! Make all the sound effects to stretch mouths and faces.

PHYSICAL WARM-UP 1: Gentle warm-up – loosen up and get rid of tension with a range of whole-body movements.

AL SAYS

" This song will make a great performance piece – ideal for assemblies. Follow our suggestions or add your own ideas and you will have a ready-made band plus singers who can sign along to the song! "

SING!

★ After warming up, play the track again and encourage the children to join in with the chorus. Can they copy the signs while they sing?

★ Teach the song using call and response (see p. 6). Start with the chorus, then move on to the verses before finishing with the middle 8 ('I wish it was raining…'). When you have finished a section, sing it through twice before moving on to the next part, checking the whole group are able to repeat it.

PLAY!

★ There is a simple glockenspiel/xylophone/chime bar part that works well in the middle 8 and final choruses of this song – it can be taught to the whole class or a small group.

★ It uses just three notes: G, F, E. As a group, find each note and play it together a few times. Make sure you hold the beaters gently so that they bounce back up from the chime bars. You'll be playing a repeating G-F-E-F pattern – the graphic score and teaching video show how it works.

★ You can play a simple, straight rhythm as indicated in the graphic score, or try something more 'jazzy' as in the video.

★ Practise the pattern slowly, with you as the leader, calling out each note in sequence ('G…F… E… F…'). Gradually build up in speed until you feel ready to try playing along with the video or an audio track.

TIP

To make it easier, you could remove all other notes on the glockenspiel/xylophone, leaving just the notes above, or use individual chime bars.

★ If you have time, allow the children to improvise and compose their own parts for the chorus and middle 8 based around the notes given. Give children the opportunity to perform their compositions to the group.

★ You have two options as to what to do after the middle 8:

  ★ If you want to have just one part, then everyone can sing the chorus twice through.

  ★ If you want to add a second part, have one group sing the middle 8 again at the same time as the others repeat the chorus. If working with mixed age groups, give the simpler middle 8 (harmony) part to the younger children. You can hear how this works on the performance track and the harmony part is also shown in the video.

  ★ Encourage both groups to increase their volume little by little to the end of the song. This develops musical part-singing through the use of dynamics.

TIP

If possible, have an adult or confident pupil leading each group to help them keep to their own part.

LEARN!

★ English: Ask the children to imagine that, like Thomas, they had woken up in the middle of the night to a room full of smoke. The next day, they write to a friend in another city to tell them what happened – what does their letter say?

★ Art & Design: Develop a class display by asking each child to draw and colour-in a typical 17th-century London house (remembering which materials would have been used). Then create flames using tissue paper to show the buildings being consumed by the fire.

SEPTEMBER 1666

(Introduction)

VERSE 1
Early in the morning at 1am
As London Town was sleeping,
A tiny spark lit the dark
And the fire it came a-creeping.

Thomas woke to thick black smoke,
He'd never seen such a thing!
They lay the blame on Pudding Lane
And the baker to the King.

CHORUS
He set it on fire – burn'd it all down,
Is that the end of London Town?
It's gone up in flames like kindling sticks,
September 1666.

VERSE 2
At the Star Inn on Fish Street Hill,
The landlord stood a-weeping.
As the wind it blew, the sparks they flew
And the flames they started leaping.

The streets were so thin, they couldn't do a thing
To stop that fire from spreading.
For three more days it blazed and blazed,
It was a nightmare they'd been dreading.

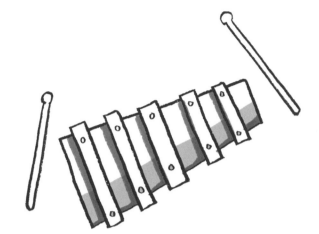

CHORUS

Set it on fire – burn'd it all down,
Is that the end of London Town?
It's gone up in flames like kindling sticks,
September 1666.

MIDDLE 8 *(x4)*
I wish it was raining and pouring
On poor old London Town.

CHORUS *(x2)*

(Melody)
Set it on fire – burn'd it all down,
Is that the end of London Town?
It's gone up in flames like kindling sticks,
September 1666.

(Harmony)
I wish it was raining and pouring
On poor old London Town.
I wish it was raining and pouring
On poor old London Town.

SWIM LITTLE FISHY, SWIM

TOPIC: Caring for our planet

CROSS-CURRICULAR LINKS: Art & Design, Design & Technology, Geography, Physical Education

A rocking blues song about how we need to clean up our oceans, recycle our plastic and not dump rubbish in the sea. Easy to learn and sing, with fun signs and a section where children can choose to mime playing an instrument in a band and rock out! Perfect for whole-school assemblies (KS1 & KS2), eco topics and letting rip!

MUSICAL LEARNING

★ Singing with expression
★ Playing untuned instruments to a steady beat
★ Exploring dynamics (volume)

RESOURCES REQUIRED

★ Teaching video
★ Performance track, backing track
★ Lyrics sheet (PDF), warm-ups sheet (PDF)
★ Optional: percussion, e.g. tambourines, wood blocks and shakers

LET'S GET STARTED...

★ To introduce the song, play the teaching video/performance track to your group. Can they begin to sing along with the chorus?

★ What do they think the song is about? Have they heard about pollution and, if they have been to the beach, have they seen this first hand?

★ Discuss any words or phrases the children may not be familiar with; for example, what is a 'litter bug'?

WARM-UP

★ Make sure your singers are sitting or standing up straight, with good posture to allow them to breathe well.

★ Choose two or three warm-ups from the PDF to help everyone to focus and get ready to sing!

AL RECOMMENDS...

LISTENING GAME 4: Follow-the-movement 'change game' – a child-led, movement-based game to focus your group's attention.

VOCAL WARM-UP 1: Gobble-de-gook – have a 'chat' with your group in *gobble-de-gook*! Move your voice up high and down low, checking that everyone makes all the sound effects to stretch their mouths and faces.

PHYSICAL WARM-UP 4: Musical statues/shapes – expand on the well-known party game to get the whole body engaged.

AL SAYS

" I am hoping this song will become an anthem for schools and children to encourage their families to recycle and look after our planet. "

SING!

★ After warming up, play the video/track again and encourage the children to join in with the chorus. Invite them to make up their own 'scrubbing' dance-move using one or both hands!

★ Go through the chorus a line at a time using the call-and-response method (see p. 6). Did everyone spot the sign for 'clean' in the phrase 'clean it up'? Pay attention to the last line, 'nothing worse than a litter bug' to make sure the children are signing correctly.

★ Now teach the first verse in the same way. Once secure, sing the whole verse through before moving on to the next section.

★ Note the subtle difference between the signs for 'clear' and 'clean'. Ensure you watch the video closely to follow the signs and demonstrate them clearly to your group.

TIP The lyrics in brackets in Verse 2 are optional – older children may like to add these parts in, but focus on learning the main lyrics first.

PLAY!

★ In the last verse, invite children to choose an instrument they might find in a rock band and mime playing it while singing the repeating line, 'There's nothing worse than a litter bug!' in their finest wild rock voices (taking care not to shout)! Try to keep everyone moving in time with the music.

★ Note that the volume needs to drop for the final line, 'So we'll have to clean it up'. You may need to signal to the group when to stop!

★ There's plenty of scope for untuned percussion to be played throughout. If you wish to use percussion, split your group into smaller groups and hand out a mixture of percussion instruments such as tambourines, wood blocks and shakers.

★ There are some percussion suggestions on the teaching video, but feel free to adapt this to suit your selection of instruments and what your group would like to play. There is no right or wrong with this song!

★ If you choose to follow the video, you'll see that both instruments mostly play along to the '1, 2, 3, 4' beat. The tambourine plays in the choruses, middle 8 and interludes following each chorus. You can add variation by putting in some rattles, as shown in the video.

★ The wood blocks play in the verses from verse 2 onwards, and in the middle 8 and final chorus.

★ If you wish to use body percussion instead, why not clap along, or use a mixture of stamping, hands on laps and clapping.

LEARN!

★ Physical Education: Invite the children to complete the movements in this energetic song by inventing their own dance-moves for the instrumental sections, based around swimming strokes and water-themed actions.

★ Design & Technology: Make shakers from recycled plastic bottles for the children to play as percussion – a practical way to reinforce the song's message!

★ Art & Design: Ask the class to design happy fish/sad fish diagrams, the first showing fish in lovely, clean water; the second displaying the fish in a polluted, litter-filled ocean. They could cut out the fish and litter and put them on sticks to hold up – great if you are sharing the song in assembly.

SWIM LITTLE FISHY, SWIM

(8-beat count-in)

INTRODUCTION *(x3)*
(Ooh-ooh)

VERSE 1
Swim little fishy, swim!
"But what am I swimming in?"
The ocean is not a bin
So why'd you throw your rubbish in?

CHORUS
We're gonna rub-a-dub, scrub-a-dub and clean it up!
We're gonna rub-a-dub, scrub-a-dub and clean it up!
We're gonna rub-a-dub, scrub-a-dub and clean it up!
Because there's nothing worse than a litter bug!

Interlude *(x3)*
(Ooh-ooh)

VERSE 2
Well, what would your mama say? (She'd say)
"I didn't bring you up this way." (No way!)
You gotta throw your rubbish away (Throw it away!)
And recycle for another day. (Recycle!)

CHORUS
We're gonna rub-a-dub, scrub-a-dub and clean it up!
We're gonna rub-a-dub, scrub-a-dub and clean it up!
We're gonna rub-a-dub, scrub-a-dub and clean it up!
There's nothing worse than a litter bug!

Interlude *(x3)*
(Ooh-ooh)

VERSE 3
Now listen: eight million tonnes a year
Is dumped in the sea, I fear.
But now that we know, it's clear
We gotta make it disappear.

CHORUS
We're gonna rub-a-dub, scrub-a-dub and clean it up!
We're gonna rub-a-dub, scrub-a-dub and clean it up!
We're gonna rub-a-dub, scrub-a-dub and clean it up!
Because there's nothing worse than a litter bug!

Interlude
(Ooh-ooh)
(Ooh-ooh)

MIDDLE 8
There's nothing worse than a litter bug!
There's nothing worse than a litter bug!
There's nothing worse than a litter bug!
So we'll have to clean it up!

CHORUS
Rub-a-dub, scrub-a-dub and clean it up!
Rub-a-dub, scrub-a-dub and clean it up!
Rub-a-dub, scrub-a-dub and clean it up!
Because there's nothing worse than a litter bug!

THERE'S A BEAR IN MY WARDROBE

TOPIC: Bears, dreams and imagination

CROSS-CURRICULAR LINKS: English, Art & Design, Physical Education

A funny song about an imaginary friendly bear who lives in your wardrobe. It features fun signs and spooky sound effects and is great fun for your bear topic or as a singing assembly. A good song to encourage reluctant singers.

MUSICAL LEARNING

★ Singing with expression

★ Making a range of sounds with voices

★ Exploring dynamics (volume)

★ Exploring and combining sounds

RESOURCES REQUIRED

★ Teaching video

★ Performance track, backing track

★ Lyrics sheet (PDF), warm-ups sheet (PDF)

★ Optional: handheld percussion, e.g. individual chime bars, rain sticks, thunder drums; assorted items that make sounds, e.g. tin foil, scrunching paper, a tray with sand or gravel

LET'S GET STARTED...

★ To introduce the song, play the teaching video/performance track to your group. What did everyone think of the song? Which were their favourite parts?

★ Ensure everyone understands all the words and phrases. Explain that this is an imaginary story: there is *not really* a bear in their wardrobe, he is an imaginary friend.

★ You could see if anyone has an imaginary friend or a cuddly soft toy they like to snuggle at night. The bear in the song is like that: he helps if they wake up in the night or have a bad dream.

WARM-UP

★ Make sure your singers are sitting or standing up straight, with good posture to allow them to breathe well.

★ Choose two or three warm-ups from the PDF to help everyone to focus and get ready to sing!

AL RECOMMENDS...

LISTENING GAME 5: Rainstorm circle – a calm listening exercise to focus your group and set the scene for a soundscape.

VOCAL WARM-UP 4: The moody song – singing a familiar song in a range of moods. Make sure creepy/spooky/scary is in there, and ensure they use their faces and bodies to emphasise the feelings.

PHYSICAL WARM-UP 3: Wobbly chicken – counting and moving in time to a beat. You can speed up the tempo as you do a couple of rounds.

SING!

★ After warming up, play the track again and encourage the children to join in with the sound effects and the chorus ('Good night, sleep tight. Don't let the bed bugs bite!').

★ Encourage them to explore different dynamics: try starting very quietly, then get louder to the end of the chorus. Make sure they don't shout the word 'bite' – this may take some practice!

★ Next, teach the whole song using the call-and-response method (see p. 6).

★ Sing through each verse at least twice before moving on to the next section, making sure everyone can sing and sign the words correctly.

★ When the children have learned all the verses, sing the entire song through.

PLAY!

★ Introduce the idea of a 'soundscape' (painting a picture or telling a story with sound) and explain that you're going to create a 'spooky soundscape' based on the lyrics of the song. You may like to display the lyrics to prompt ideas for spooky sounds!

★ Divide into small groups and choose some percussion instruments, individual chime bars, and/or items that make sounds.

★ Allow the children to explore the sounds their instruments make for a few minutes.

★ Explain that you will show them when to play by pointing at their group, and indicate if they should play quietly or loudly with your hand movements (hands getting wider apart for louder, hands moving together for quieter). When your hands touch, the sounds should stop!

★ Give the children the opportunity to play the 'conductor' role, pointing at different groups and moving their hands together and apart. They may find it easier to focus on the two elements separately at first.

TIP

Once you've created something you're all happy with, you can use your soundscape piece to set the scene before singing the song!

LEARN!

★ English: Discuss what each of your instruments or sound-makers might represent and write your collective ideas down for everyone to see. Invite the children to write short stories that include some of these elements, then read out the stories with the appropriate sound effects.

★ Art & Design/Physical Education: Ask the children to 'invent' a monster on paper. Then ask them to think about the character they've drawn. How does it move? What sounds does it make? Bring the drawings to life by moving around like your characters in the song interludes.

AL SAYS

“ I often demonstrate how much spookier something can sound if you read or sing it in a hushed voice. Choose a line from the song and ask your group to sing it once in their 'normal' voice, then again in a hushed almost-whisper and see what they think. Changing their voices like this introduces singing with expression and dynamics. „

THERE'S A BEAR IN MY WARDROBE

(Introduction)

VERSE 1

There's a bear in my wardrobe and every night
I give him crisps and juice and cuddle him tight.
We play hide and seek, and he always lets me win
Then he reads me a story and tucks me in.

CHORUS

He says: Good night, sleep tight.
Don't let the bed bugs bite!

(Interlude)

VERSE 2

I thought I heard a monster yawn. (Rahhhh!)
I think he's under my bed. (Eeeek!)
My bear jumped out and wrestled him down
And now the monster's dead! (Hooray!)

VERSE 3

I thought I heard a floor board creak. (Creeeeak!)
I think there's a ghost in here. (Ooooo!)
The bear jumped out and chased it away
So now I can go back to sleep! (Snore!)

CHORUS

He says: Good night, sleep tight.
Don't let the bed bugs bite!
Don't let the bed bugs bite!
(slow) **Don't let the bed bugs bite!**

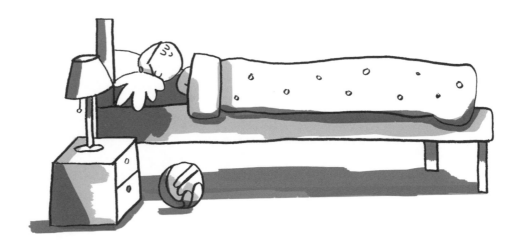

WHATEVER THE WEATHER

TOPIC: Weather and seasons

CROSS-CURRICULAR LINKS: Art & Design, Geography

A cheerful, up-tempo song about playing outside, whatever the weather may be! This song is easy to learn and teaches the makaton signs for the seasons, weather and activities you can do outdoors. Great for singing assembly and weather topics.

MUSICAL LEARNING

★ Singing in unison
★ Playing untuned instruments musically
★ Exploring and combining sounds

RESOURCES REQUIRED

★ Teaching video
★ Performance track, backing track
★ Lyrics sheet (PDF), warm-ups sheet (PDF)
★ Optional: any untuned percussion (e.g. drums), percussion grid (PDF), tuned percussion (e.g. chime bars and beaters, xylophones), items to make weather sound effects for soundscape (rainsticks, thunder drums, scrunched paper and stiff card/wobble boards)

LET'S GET STARTED...

★ To introduce the song, play the teaching video/performance track to your group. Discuss the words and phrases to ensure everyone understands the song.

★ Can the children remember the signs for each season? What does the sign for 'day is dawning' represent? (the sun rising).

★ Can they remember what activities the song mentioned for hot and cold weather? What do they like to do in different seasons?

WARM-UP

★ Make sure your singers are sitting or standing up straight, with good posture to allow them to breathe well.

★ Choose two or three warm-ups from the PDF to help everyone to focus and get ready to sing!

AL RECOMMENDS...

LISTENING GAME 2: Don't clap this one back – a short, snappy listening exercise to grab everyone's attention. Introduce 'Now be a statue' as an adaptation of this.

VOCAL WARM-UP 5: Tongue Twisters – get mouths and voices ready for lots of words!

PHYSICAL WARM-UP 5: A four- or eight-beat dance – choose four or eight different moves to go in sequence as you move to a beat or clap along.

SING!

★ After warming up, play the track again and encourage the children to join in with the chorus.

★ Can they copy the signs while they sing, and can they clap and 'slurp' in the right places?

TIP

Before you start, go through the signs for the seasons one at a time.

★ Teach the chorus as a call and response (see p. 6). Make sure everyone is able to sing and sign correctly, and practise getting the rhythm of the claps right.

★ Once secure, sing the chorus twice through, and then learn the verses in the same way.

★ Sing the whole song through!

PLAY!

★ Try playing the two claps in the chorus (after 'everyone') on any untuned percussion instrument (e.g. wood blocks, drums) or using other body percussion. The claps are demonstrated in the orange window on the teaching video.

★ Lay out your percussion instruments and allow the children to select their own. Once everyone has chosen one, sing the song together, adding percussion in place of the claps.

★ Now have everyone choose a new instrument before playing the song again. You could even split into groups and form an 'arrangement' by together deciding which instruments will play in each of the three choruses.

★ For an additional challenge, invite two groups of children to add drums and finger taps.

★ The drummers should play on beat 1 through the introduction and choruses and the finger tappers should play on beats 2 and 4 throughout the verses and interludes (starting after the first chorus), and at the very end.

★ Watch the teaching video and refer to the percussion grid to see how these fit together.

LEARN!

★ Music: Create a weather soundscape using a combination of instruments such as chime bars, xylophones, djembe drums, shakers, scrapers, thunder drums and rainsticks. These can be used alongside voices and other items that make weather-type sounds, such as scrunched paper or marbles being rolled round in a tin. Try describing sunny, windy, rainy, stormy and snowy weather.

TIP

Use Listening Game 5 (Rainstorm circle) to introduce the idea of building up weather sounds.

★ Art & design: Display the lyrics of the song. Divide the group into four and allocate each a season. Ask each child to draw one aspect associated with their season (such as a green tree or ice-cream for summer). Help the pupils cut out their drawings and then create a collage for each season; this could be displayed in the classroom or held up at the appropriate moment when performing the song.

AL SAYS

" When the children know this song well, encourage them to sing expressively. For example, the Autumn/Winter verse could be sung at low volume, with 'chilly' voices, then they could sing loudly and excitedly for 'we'll go sledging in the park – wheeee!'. "

WHATEVER THE WEATHER

(Introduction)

CHORUS
The day is dawning, it's just begun,
What will the weather be for everyone? *(clap, clap)*
It's early morning, it's just begun,
Whatever the weather, we're going to have some fun!

(Interlude)

VERSE 1
Spring is the season the plants start to grow,
The sun comes out and melts all the snow.
Summer's even hotter, the trees are really green,
We eat the biggest ice-cream our eyes have ever seen! (slurp, slurp, slurp)

CHORUS
The day is dawning, it's just begun,
What will the weather be for everyone? *(clap, clap)*
It's early morning, it's just begun,
Whatever the weather, we're going to have some fun!

(Interlude)

VERSE 2

Autumn takes the leaves and blows them to the ground,
So we can make a pile, we love that crunching sound.
Winter time is chilly, the afternoons get dark,
We all wish for snow and we'll go sledging in the park! (Wheeee!)

CHORUS

The day is dawning, it's just begun,
What will the weather be for everyone? *(clap, clap)*
It's early morning, it's just begun,
Whatever the weather, we're going to have some fun!

OUTRO

Whatever the weather, we're going to have some fun!
Whatever the weather, we're going to have some fun!
… Some fun!

WHEELS GO ROUND

TOPIC: Transport and family

**CROSS-CURRICULAR LINKS: Art & Design, Design & Technology;
Drama, Physical Education**

This catchy song makes a pleasant alternative to 'Wheels on the bus'. It is repetitive and easy for young children to learn and sing, featuring plenty of humour, action-packed signs and sound effects for exploring different vocal qualities. A fun song for a transport topic or use it in any singing assembly from Reception class upwards.

MUSICAL LEARNING

★ Singing in unison
★ Making a range of sounds with voices
★ Playing untuned instruments musically

RESOURCES REQUIRED

★ Teaching video
★ Performance track, backing track
★ Lyrics sheet (PDF), warm-ups sheet (PDF)
★ Optional: percussion, e.g. shakers, tambourines, percussion grid (PDF)

LET'S GET STARTED...

★ To introduce the song, play the teaching video/performance track to your group. Are they able to start joining in with the chorus and copy some of the signs? Can they make the car noises?

★ What modes of transport were mentioned in the song? Can they sign them to you?

★ Discuss any words or phrases the children may not be familiar with. For example, in verse 2, what does 'She sometimes lets us ride for free' mean? In verse 3, why does the uncle have 'breakfast in America and teatime in Tibet'? (He flies his plane around the world!)

WARM-UP

★ Make sure your singers are sitting or standing up straight, with good posture to allow them to breathe well.

★ Choose two or three warm-ups from the PDF to help everyone to focus and get ready to sing!

AL RECOMMENDS...

LISTENING GAME 2: Don't clap this one back – a short, snappy listening exercise to grab everyone's attention. Introduce 'Now be a statue' (Listening Game 3) as an adaptation of this.

VOCAL WARM-UP 2: Drive the car – travel up high and down low in your car/truck/motorcycle, making 'brmm' sound effects to stretch mouths and faces.

PHYSICAL WARM-UP 3: Wobbly chicken – a funny warm-up to get children moving and thinking about rhythm and pulse. Speed up for additional warmth!

AL SAYS

" Before singing this song, I always ask the children to look for their (imaginary) keys, get in their car, buckle up, start the engine and go for a drive around. This really gets them in the zone! "

SING!

★ After warming up, play the track again and encourage the children to join in with the chorus. Can they copy the signs while they sing along?

★ Encourage plenty of vocal sound effects for the engine, horn and brakes.

★ Teach the chorus using call and response (see p. 6). Once secure, sing it twice through before learning the verses in the same way.

★ Make sure everyone is able to sing and sign the words correctly.

★ Once you've taught each verse, sing it through twice and with the chorus before moving to the next one.

★ Sing the whole song through from beginning to end when you have learned all the verses.

★ When singing to the backing track, listen out for the four taps that signal the entry into the verse at 0:08.

TIP

Encourage the children to use funny voices, pull faces and make noises on the funny bits such as 'D'oh, Dad!', 'Hello down there!', Granny's bumpy tractor and the car noises in the chorus. This will encourage singing with expression and will prove irresistible to reluctant or nervous singers.

PLAY!

★ If you want to add some percussion to this song, there are two simple percussion parts on the teaching video that you could try.

★ Split your group into three and have the first group sing and sign.

★ The second group plays shakers on the beat in the choruses.

★ The third group plays tambourines on the beat in the choruses, just like the shakers, but they can also add a hand tap on '2' and '4' to create a cool shake-tap-shake-tap pattern. The percussion grid shows how the parts fit together.

★ Note that the percussion patterns change for 'The horn goes beep! The brakes go squeak!': there's a rattle followed by taps/shakes on 'beep' and 'squeak'. You can see this demonstrated in the teaching video.

★ Encourage everyone to follow the video, supporting them to start and stop in the correct places and watch carefully to help them get the rhythm right.

★ The percussion is different in the last verse: rather than playing to the beat, shake your tambourines and shakers as on the video.

★ Rotate the groups so that everyone has a turn playing each instrument and singing/signing.

TIP

Ask an adult or confident child from each group to stand at the front and lead their group.

LEARN!

★ Design & Technology: Ask the children to invent and draw their own amazing super-vehicle, adding labels to explain the features (horn, breaks, wings, etc.).

★ Art & Design: Invite children to draw details from each verse (e.g. Dad in a racing car,

Mum driving a bus). You could photograph the pictures and play a slideshow while performing the song.

★ Drama/Dance: If performing the song, children could dress up and play the roles in each verse and make cut-outs of each vehicle!

WHEELS GO ROUND

(Introduction)

VERSE 1

My dad drives a sports car
Around the motorway,
He drives it really fast, yeah,
But he always goes the wrong way! (D'oh, Dad!)

CHORUS

And the wheels go round and round and round,
And the engine makes a 'brrm-brrm' sound.
The horn goes beep!
The brakes go squeak!
How will we get to school this week?

VERSE 2

My mum drives a bus, yeah,
She does it for her job.
She sometimes lets us ride for free,
We love it up the top! (Hello down there!)

CHORUS

And the wheels go round and round and round,
And the engine makes a 'brrm-brrm' sound.
The horn goes beep!
The brakes go squeak!
How will we get to school this week?

VERSE 3

My uncle drives an aeroplane,
He flies a jumbo jet!
He has his breakfast in America
And teatime in Tibet. (Cheers, everybody!)

CHORUS

And the wheels go round and round and round,
And the engine makes a 'brrm-brrm' sound.
The horn goes beep!
The brakes go squeak!
How will we get to school this week?

VERSE 4

My granny drives a tractor
Down a bumpy track.
She lets me sit up front with her
And the dog goes in the back. (Woof woof!)

FINAL CHORUS

And the wheels go round and round and round,
And the engine makes a 'brrm-brrm' sound.
The horn goes beep!
The brakes go squeak!
How will we get to school this week?

If the wheels go round and round and round,
And the engine makes a 'brrm-brrm' sound.
The horn goes beep!
The brakes go squeak!
How will we get to school this week?
How will we get to school this week?
How will we get to school this week?
Hmm, I think we'd better use our feet!

Curriculum grid

The Key Stage 1 attainment targets are outlined at the top of the grid below. By simply listening to and singing these songs, children will be well on their way to ticking many of the boxes, particularly those associated with using voices expressively and listening to high-quality recorded music.

We've indicated which songs will help you achieve other targets when following the guidance offered in the notes (summarised in the 'Musical Learning' sections). You may find it useful to refer to this grid when reflecting on the areas you've already addressed, and those you'd like to work on.

Song title	Pupils should be taught to:			
	use their voices expressively and creatively by singing songs and speaking chants and rhymes	play tuned and untuned instruments musically	listen with concentration and understanding to a range of high-quality live and recorded music	experiment with, create, select and combine sounds using the inter-related dimensions of music*
Big Red Barn	★	★	★	★
The Dinosaur Dance	★	★	★	★
Friend to the End	★		★	★
Go Santa Go!	★	★	★	★
I Love Cake!	★	★	★	
A Pirate Adventure	★	★	★	★
The Seed and the Tree	★	★	★	★
September 1666	★	★	★	★
Swim Little Fishy, Swim	★	★	★	
There's a Bear in my Wardrobe	★	★		★
Whatever the Weather	★	★	★	★
Wheels Go Round	★	★	★	

*The inter-related dimensions of music: pitch, duration, dynamics, tempo, timbre, texture, structure and appropriate musical notations